BACK FROM NEAR EXTINCTION

BALD EAGLE

by Anita Yasuda

Content Consultant
James W. Grier
Emeritus Professor
Department of Biological Sciences
North Dakota State University

Core Library

An Imprint of Abdo Publishing
abdopublishing.com

abdopublishing.com

Published by Abdo Publishing, a division of ABDO, PO Box 398166, Minneapolis, Minnesota 55439. Copyright © 2017 by Abdo Consulting Group, Inc. International copyrights reserved in all countries. No part of this book may be reproduced in any form without written permission from the publisher. Core Library™ is a trademark and logo of Abdo Publishing.

Printed in the United States of America, North Mankato, Minnesota
082016
012017

Cover Photo: Peter Wey/Shutterstock Images
Interior Photos: Peter Wey/Shutterstock Images, 1; Richard Fitzer/Shutterstock Images, 4; iStockphoto, 9, 45; Menno Schaefer/Shutterstock Images, 12, 18; Alexey Pushkin/Shutterstock Images, 15; Red Line Editorial, 16; Charlie Neibergall/AP Images, 20, 43; Marion Owen/Newscom, 22; Shutterstock Images, 25; Ben Margot/AP Images, 27; Bo Rader/Wichita Eagle/TNS/Newscom, 30, 37; University Of Tennessee/ZumaPress/Newscom, 33; Ian Duffield/Shutterstock Images, 39

Editor: Megan Anderson
Series Designer: Jake Nordby

Publisher's Cataloging-in-Publication Data

Names: Yasuda, Anita, author.
Title: Bald eagle / by Anita Yasuda.
Description: Minneapolis, MN : Abdo Publishing, 2017. | Series: Back from near
     extinction | Includes bibliographical references and index.
Identifiers: LCCN 2016945424 | ISBN 9781680784640 (lib. bdg.) |
     ISBN 9781680798494 (ebook)
Subjects: LCSH: Bald eagle--Juvenile literature.
Classification: DDC 598.9--dc23
LC record available at http://lccn.loc.gov/2016945424

CONTENTS

CHAPTER ONE

HISTORY OF THE BALD EAGLE

I n the gray mist, an eagle perches on top of a tall tree. His bright white head and tail feathers stand out from the bare winter branches. The icy waters below are filled with salmon. Using his sharp eyes, the eagle watches as fish push their bodies upstream. Eager for breakfast, the eagle glides from the tree. He circles the river using his tail to steer. Spying a salmon stuck on a moss-covered rock,

Chemicals and hunting once threatened the bald eagle population with extinction.

the eagle swoops down. His knifelike claws, called talons, snatch at the fish. But the fish is too heavy for the eagle to carry away. The eagle drops it at a slippery log nearby. In the distance, the eagle hears the cries of its chicks. Quickly, he rips off a small piece of the salmon and flies back to feed his young.

As the fog lifts, sunlight pours into the valley. The wind begins to rise. The eagle's mate leaves the nest to soar on currents of air over the land. Her shadow falls on the mountains. Their caps sparkle under the

National Symbol

In 1776 the United States was a new nation. The US Congress wanted a seal design it could use on important papers. The design would represent the country's new government. Over the next six years, there were many different ideas. In 1782 the bald eagle became the national bird of the United States. That year Congress also agreed to the design for the nation's seal that is still used today. The seal shows a bald eagle with its wings stretched wide. On its breast is the American flag. An olive branch in one claw represents peace. Arrows in the other claw represent war.

new snow. By midmorning, eagles are everywhere. They fill the air. Most are eager to feed on the salmon. They cry and shriek as they fight over the fish. When they leave, every bone will be picked clean.

The bald eagle is found almost entirely in North America. Many native people saw the eagle as a symbol of peace and strength. They admired its hunting skills. Tribes such as the Sioux used eagle feathers as part of their religion. The Tlingit of Alaska used its image on totem poles. In 1782, when Americans needed a symbol for their new nation, they chose the bald eagle. It stood for freedom and liberty. At this time, there may have been as many as half a million eagles. They lived in almost every state.

Eagles at Risk

Not everyone felt the eagle was a special bird. Many early settlers believed it ate their livestock. They began killing eagles in large numbers. Over the next 200 years, the eagle faced more threats from humans. Humans shot and trapped eagles, and

Eagle Species

There are more than 60 kinds of eagles in the world. North America is home to two species. They are the golden eagle and the bald eagle. They are similar in size and appearance, but their color and markings are different. The body of the golden eagle is light brown or dark brown. Adults do not have any white markings. This eagle also has golden-colored feathers on its crown and neck. The bald eagle lives near water. But the golden eagle doesn't need to live near water. Golden eagles live in drier areas, such as plains and mountains. Golden eagles are also found in Europe, Asia, and parts of Africa.

nests were destroyed. The US Congress passed legislation to protect the bald eagle in 1940. But the shooting continued. Chemicals, such as lead, also poisoned eagles.

By the 1960s, there were fewer than 500 pairs of eagles in the lower 48 states. In 1967 the bald eagle was named an endangered species. There was only a slim hope the bald eagle population would survive. The government passed new laws. These laws further protected bald eagles and their nests.

A bald eagle's sharp talons help it catch fish swimming beneath the surface of the water.

Conservation groups also found ways to help. They worked to educate the public about eagles. They also protected eagle nesting areas. In time, bald eagle numbers grew. Because of these efforts, the eagle was taken off the Endangered Species List in 2007.

Jon Gerrard and Gary Bortolotti wrote *The Bald Eagle: Haunts and Habits of a Wilderness Monarch*. In their book, they write about the history of the bald eagle in North America:

> *Bald Eagles were present in North America when Europeans first arrived. The eagles nested on both coasts and along every major river and large lake in the interior from Florida to Baja California in the south and from Labrador to Alaska in the north. In many areas, they were abundant. . . .*
>
> *There were between a quarter million and a half million Bald Eagles on the continent. . . . As settlement moved west across the continent, farms and ranches began to appear. . . . The countryside swarmed with people with guns. A threat to livestock or the collection of a trophy was excuse for some marksmen; an easy target was good enough for others. Traps set for wolves sometimes caught eagles.*
>
> Source: Jon M. Gerrard and Gary R. Bortolotti. The Bald Eagle: Haunts and Habits of a Wilderness Monarch. *Washington, DC: Smithsonian Institution, 1988. Print. 15–16.*

What's the Big Idea?

Take a close look at what the authors wrote. What is their main idea? Write a few sentences describing this idea. Include two or three pieces of evidence they use to support this point.

CHAPTER TWO

ABOUT THE BALD EAGLE

B ald eagles are powerful raptors. As adults, their wings span nearly 7 feet (2.1 m). They use these strong wings to fly up to 75 miles per hour (120 km/h) when diving for food. Male eagles are 30 to 35 inches (76–89 cm) tall and weigh 8 to 10 pounds (3.6–4.5 kg). Like most birds of prey, females are larger than males. Females are 34 to 43 inches (86–109 cm) tall and weigh

Eagles don't acquire the white feathers on their heads until the age of four or five.

A Chick's Life

When a baby eagle is born, it weighs only a few ounces. A chick needs its parents to feed it until it is approximately five weeks old. Adult eagles rip meat into smaller pieces for their young. Chicks will eat as much as they can. They store extra food in their crop. A crop is a sac in an eagle's neck. Adult eagles can store up to 1.5 pounds (0.68 kg) of food in their crops.

10 to 14 pounds (4.5–6.4 kg). Both have dark brown feathers over their bodies and wings. Their heads and tails are white. This is where the name *bald* comes from. An old meaning of *bald* is "marked with white."

Baby eagles are known as eaglets. Eaglets have light whitish-gray feathers called down when they first hatch. These are replaced by darker down feathers. Then the main feathers begin to develop. During their first year, young bald eagles vary from mostly brown to black in color. By age four or five, they have adult feathers, a white head and tail, and a dark brown body.

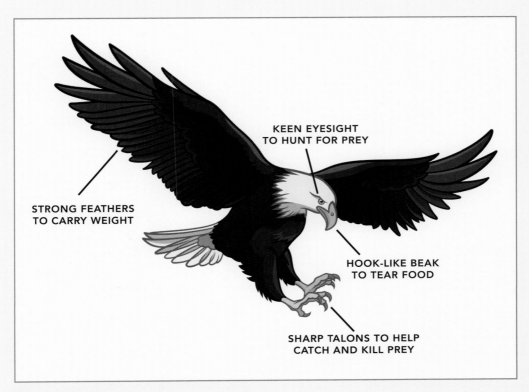

Bald Eagle
This diagram shows the different characteristics of a bald eagle. How does its physical characteristics help it survive in the wild? Which characteristics make it such an effective hunter?

All eagles have sharp beaks and talons to catch prey. Bald eagles also use their clear, accurate eyesight to hunt. They can see about two and a half times better than humans.

Eagles may eat up to 1.5 pounds (0.68 kg) or more of food a day. Fish is the bald eagle's main

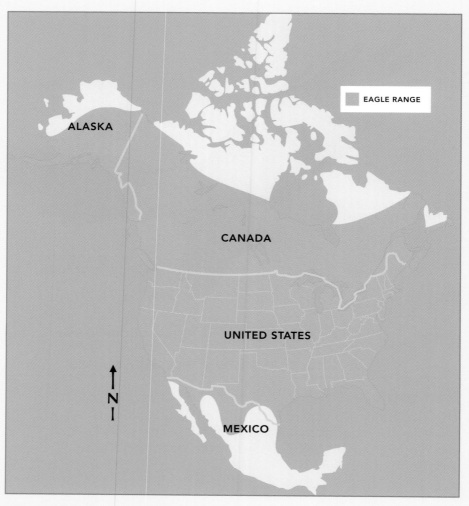

The Bald Eagle's Range
This map shows the large range of the bald eagle. Why do you think these areas are good places for bald eagles to live? Use information from this chapter to support your answer.

source of food. This is why eagles live near water.

Bald eagles belong to a group known as "sea eagles." Some return each year by the hundreds to rivers where salmon spawn. Eagles also eat waterfowl, other birds, and small- to medium-sized mammals such as squirrels and muskrats. Animals hit by cars or shot by hunters, such as deer, are also important food to eagles.

The Eagle's Home

There are approximately 250,000 or more bald eagles in North America today. There are so many now, experts are not sure of their exact number. They are found from coast to coast. Alaska has one of the largest populations, with approximately 50,000 living in the state. Eagles are also common in British Columbia. Some eagles live across Canada's northern forests.

Eagles may move south in the winter depending on the local food supply. Many of them stay around their nests throughout the year. They nest along oceans, lakes, and rivers, such as the Mississippi and Missouri.

Male eagles tend to have higher-pitched calls compared to female eagles.

The best habitats have large, strong trees. Trees need to be strong to hold the weight of an eagle's nest. Pairs of eagles often return to the same nest for several years. They spend several months tending to their nest. They add sticks to it and line it with reeds, grass, moss, and other soft vegetation. Nests can weigh up to 1,000 pounds (453.5 kg). The largest bald eagle nest on record, in Florida, measured more than 9 feet (2.7 m) across and 20 feet (6 m) deep. In areas with no trees, eagles may nest in cliffs. Rock spires or large cacti are also used for nesting. From these high perches, eagles watch for prey in the distance and will chase off other birds to defend their territory.

Mating

Between the ages of four and six, bald eagles start producing offspring. In the spring, eagles begin to look for mates. They call to one another and swoop and dive through the air. They will grab talons and spin quickly toward the ground before letting go at the last minute. This action is called cartwheeling. The male and female eagle might stay together for several years or occasionally change mates. If a mate dies or moves on to another mate, the other may look for a new mate.

Once a female has mated, it may lay up to

Smooth Feathers

Approximately 7,000 feathers cover an adult bald eagle. Like other birds, the eagle can move each feather one by one. This allows the eagle to flatten its feathers to fly or fluff its feathers to keep warm. The eagle has a special oil gland near its tail. It uses its beak to apply the oil to its feathers. The oil protects the feathers from water.

After bringing food back for its eaglets, a bald eagle flies away from its nest.

three eggs. Each egg is about the size of a tennis ball. Both mother and father eagles take turns sitting on the eggs. The eggs must be kept warm and safe from predators. Animals such as raccoons or bears will sometimes try to eat the eggs or small young. Birds such as ravens, crows, or gulls are also threats to young eagles. Owls might try to take over the nest.

The eagle chicks hatch in 34 to 36 days. Chicks are not able to take their first flight until they are approximately 10 to 12 weeks old. But many of these chicks do not live. Chicks hatch in the order the eggs are laid and are usually born two days apart. Often, the older chick will attack the younger one or take its food. Scientists estimate that only 70 percent of all eagles survive their first year.

EXPLORE ONLINE

The focus of Chapter Two was on characteristics of the bald eagle. The website below has more information on the bald eagle. As you know, every source is different. How is the information on the website different from the information in this chapter? What information is the same? How do the two sources present information differently?

National Geographic Kids: Bald Eagle
mycorelibrary.com/bald-eagle

THREATS TO BALD EAGLES

Starting in the 1700s, the biggest danger to bald eagles was from people. Farms and towns took over areas where eagles lived. There were no laws at this time to stop people from cutting down trees or shooting eagles. Trees provide important places for eagles to rest and build nests. And like eagles, settlers preferred to live near water. Eagles need to be close to rivers or lakes to find fish

Pollution, poisoning, and hunting posed major threats to the eagle population.

and other prey. People needed water for their families and animals. They also used it to help their crops grow. Soon, many waterways became busy with boats. But eagles could not avoid people. People frequently shot the eagles.

Shooting was a major threat to eagles. People shot not only eagles but also animals that made up their food supply. Hunters trapped animals such as muskrats and other fur bearers. They also took a toll on large game, such as deer, elk, and bison. Eagles once took advantage of the large herds of bison in the West. They did not prey on large mammals such as bison. But they fed on them once they died. Bald eagles eat carrion, or dead meat that is still fresh. Bison were likely a favorite source of carrion. But in the mid-1800s, settlers and hunters from the cities began shooting bison for sport. This caused eagles to lose that source of food.

Eagles were killed by shooting and trapping. Their nests were destroyed. And their food sources

Hunters not only targeted bald eagles, but threatened their food supply as well.

Bounties

In 1917 the bald eagle bounty in Alaska was 50 cents for each dead bird. By 1923 it rose to one dollar. Eagle hunting became a big business. Some hunters earned several hundred dollars a year. Settler Josephine Sather boasted of killing approximately 200 eagles. She said she shot them to protect her fox farm. The Alaskan law against eagles lasted for 36 years. The bounty finally ended in 1953.

were reduced. Over time, eagle populations started to decline.

Fear of Bald Eagles

In the 1800s, people did not know a lot about bald eagles. Eagles scared many settlers. Stories spread of eagles taking children. Some people believed eagles killed livestock. Newspapers reported eagles taking goats and chickens from settlers' pens. These stories were not true. But it did not stop people from killing eagles out of fear.

People also shot eagles for sport. In some areas of the West and Alaska, states urged people to shoot eagles. Eagles were considered a threat to fishing,

Three-day-old chicks are cared for by experts after hatching from DDT contaminated eggs.

pets, fur farming, and even to people themselves. Lawmakers offered money for each eagle killed. From 1917 to 1953, more than 120,000 bald eagles were shot. The bounty was removed in 1953.

Poisoning

After World War II (1939–1945), eagles faced a new threat. People began using a new chemical to kill insects. It was called DDT. People used it to kill bugs,

No More DDT

Rachel Carson was a writer and scientist. She first became interested in nature as a young child. In 1962 Carson wrote the book *Silent Spring*. In her book, she discussed the use of pesticides such as DDT. Carson believed they hurt the environment. Because of her book, the public became aware of these dangers. Many were shocked. They did not know pesticides were killing off birds such as the bald eagle. As a result, the public encouraged the government to take action.

such as mosquitoes. Mosquitoes can carry human diseases, including malaria. Farmers sprayed DDT on their fields and crops. It was also used along shorelines to get rid of other pests. Families used it around their homes and on their lawns.

DDT was good at killing insects. But it also hurt the environment and was a danger to bald eagles. DDT takes a long time to break down. Eventually, it washed off the land and into the water system. It ended up in the eagle's food cycle. Fish absorbed DDT and stored it in their bodies. Bald eagles ate the fish. Over time, high levels of DDT built up in the eagles. The poison weakened their eggshells. The thin shells caused the eggs to dry out. The shells would break, or the birds died before they hatched. This meant fewer eaglets were born. With all of these threats, eagle populations began to decline.

FURTHER EVIDENCE

Chapter Three talks about threats to bald eagles. What evidence was given to support this point? Visit the website below. Can you find the information on the website that supports the author's point? Write a few sentences about what you find.

The Bald Eagle Returns
mycorelibrary.com/bald-eagle

CHAPTER FOUR

SAVING THE BALD EAGLE

By the 1920s, bald eagle populations were still dropping. Members of the American Ornithologists' Union (AOU) became worried. They disagreed with bounties put on bald eagles. The group took steps to save the eagle. They began warning the public through the media. The group wrote articles explaining how the eagle population was threatened. The AOU also used the media to

A biologist picks up a young bald eagle after it jumped from its nest in Kansas.

clear up myths about the bald eagle. It explained eagles did not attack livestock like many people believed. But eagles did eat dead or dying animals. The AOU warned if nothing was done, the bald eagle would likely become extinct. The group wanted to know why there were no laws to protect the eagle. After all, the bald eagle was the United States' national symbol.

Laws for Eagles

In 1940 the US Congress took steps to save the bald eagle. It passed the Bald Eagle Act. It made it illegal to kill bald eagles. It also made it against the law to sell or even own eagles. Breaking the law could result in jail or a large fine. But the law did not initially apply to Alaska. This changed in 1959, when Alaska became a state. Congress changed the law a few years later to include the golden eagle. It became known as the Bald and Golden Eagle Protection Act.

People continued to kill eagles even though bounties were eventually eliminated, and the practice

A bald eagle is treated at the University of Tennessee after being shot.

became illegal. The eagle population continued to decline. Scientists were not sure what the cause was. Charles Broley was one of the first to make an important discovery. Broley was a Canadian with an interest in birds, particularly bald eagles. After retiring, he traveled to the United States. Broley spent time in Florida, a state with a very large population of eagles. He began studying the Florida eagles in 1939. Over ten years, he attached numbered bands to the legs of more than 1,000 bald eagles. Before Broley's work, only 166 eagles had ever been marked. The bands showed the eagles spent part of the year nesting in Florida and then often traveled north. They also showed eagles were having fewer eaglets each year. Broley thought this could be linked to DDT. He began speaking and writing on the subject.

After Broley's death in 1959, other scientists continued his work. Scientists compared the thickness of eagle shells before and after exposure to DDT. This helped them

Eagle Feathers

Under the 1940 eagle law, people are not allowed to take or own an eagle feather. But eagle feathers have been part of Native American culture for thousands of years. They are used in special religious ceremonies. Because of this, the government set up the National Eagle Repository in 1970. Dead eagles from all over the country are sent to the repository in Denver, Colorado. Some of the eagles come from zoos and wildlife agencies. After a request is received, eagle feathers or parts are then sent to tribes all over the United States.

show that DDT built up in eagles' bodies. But DDT use was not banned until December 31, 1972.

In 1973 Congress passed the Endangered Species Act (ESA). Eagles were among several species protected under the act. Conservation centers started raising eagles and releasing them back into the wild. By 1995 eagle numbers rose to approximately 4,450 pairs. In 2007 this number was more than 9,000 pairs. Scientists decided the eagle no longer needed the protection of the ESA. On June 28, 2007, the bald eagle was removed from the Endangered Species List.

New Threats

Stronger laws and public awareness helped the bald eagle make a successful comeback. There are at least 250,000 bald eagles today. Most of these eagles live in the United States and Canada. New regulations have helped protect nesting sites.

However, some threats still exist. Traps meant for other animals sometimes accidentally catch and kill eagles. Trapping regulations have greatly reduced this threat. Lead poisoning also continues to be a major threat toward eagles. Hunters often use lead shotgun pellets or rifle bullets to kill various game animals. This includes large game such as deer. Lead pellets or bullet fragments enter their bodies. Eagles often scavenge what hunters leave behind. Lead can cause eagles to lose weight and die. Other causes of eagle deaths included accidents with vehicles. Eagles flying low over highways or near airports can be hit. They are sometimes hit when feeding along roads.

Exciting Future

Eagles and people get along much better than they used to. People now work to keep these birds protected. Knowledge about eagles has helped people understand their behavior. Eagles now live close to people in both cities and rural areas.

Scientists study bald eagles so they can protect them better. Once, scientists could only study eagle nests with binoculars or telescopes. From the air, they used helicopters. Now, there are nest cameras.

A biologist in Kansas measures the beak of a bald eagle chick before it is returned to its nest.

Bands

Scientists use a tool called a band to research bald eagles. A biologist first climbs to a nest to capture an eaglet or carefully captures flying eagles with special nets. The eaglet is banded and studied in the nest or placed in a special bag and carefully lowered to the ground for study. Once on the ground, the scientists record an eagle's measurements, age, and sex. Then scientists fix a band to the eagle's leg. Each band has a number. Sometimes color bands or other markers are also attached to the bird. The Bird Banding Lab in Maryland organizes all banding in the United States. The lab relies on the public to spot banded birds. They use this data to study eagles.

The cameras show the daily lives of eagles. They allow scientists to see how eagle parents care for their eggs. At a nest camera in Washington, DC, there is a 24-hour live broadcast of one eagle family. The nest cameras have infrared technology, which allows scientists to see eagles at night. The eagles are called Mr. President and the First Lady. In 2016 the pair became parents to two chicks. There are also many other eagle

Experts hope conservation efforts will help keep the bald eagle population soaring.

nest cams. One of the most popular eagle cams is in Decorah, Iowa.

Tracking of eagle movements also enables scientists to learn more about bald eagles. Eagles are fitted with tracking devices that look like tiny backpacks. Straps fit around the sides of the birds. The units are solar powered and last approximately one to two years. Eagles in Chesapeake Bay are part of the largest study. More than 70 birds are being tracked. Scientists learning where bald eagles fly can identify hazards to the eagle population. This information can help people find ways to reduce or get rid of these dangers.

Bald eagles are doing well, but they still face risks. Eagles sometimes die from poisoning and traps. Like people, eagles need clean air and water plus safe areas to live. Government agencies and nongovernment groups work to educate the public about eagles and their nests. They hope to ensure these symbols of the United States fly in America's skies for generations to come.

Ed Britton is an environmental writer. In his article "Lead Exposure in Bald Eagles in the Upper Midwest," he writes about bald eagles dying of lead poisoning:

> *During winter, bald eagles . . . congregate along the Upper Mississippi River and other large waterways in the states of Illinois, Iowa, Wisconsin and Minnesota. Each year, dead bald eagles are found throughout the Region. . . . The liver analysis showed that 60 percent of the eagles had detectable concentrations of lead. . . . During winter months . . . eagles rely on carrion as a primary food source, especially deer carcasses and offal (gut piles) . . . after hunting events. This fact led us to focus on lead ammunition used in deer hunting as a source of lead available to eagles. Offal piles from 25 deer shot with lead ammunition were collected and radiographed. The radiographs showed that 36 percent . . . contained lead.*

> *Source: Ed Britton. "Lead Exposure in Bald Eagles in the Upper Midwest." US Fish and Wildlife Service. US Fish and Wildlife Service Midwest Region, March 2014. Web. Accessed July 1, 2016.*

What's the Big Idea?

Take a close look at Britton's words. What is his main idea? What evidence is used to support his point? Write a few sentences discussing this evidence.

SPECIES OVERVIEW

Common Name

- Bald eagle

Scientific Name

- *Haliaeetus leucocephalus*

Average Size

- Up to 38 inches (96 cm) in length; wingspan is approximately 80 inches (203 cm)
- 8–14 pounds (3.6–5.4 kg)

Color

- Adult bald eagles have dark brown bodies, white heads and tails, and yellow bills, legs, and feet.

Diet

- Fish, birds, small- to medium-sized mammals, and carrion

Average Life Span

- Approximately 40 to 50 years

Habitat

- Along the coast and near rivers, lakes, and wetlands in Canada, the United States, and northern Mexico

Threats

- Hunting and poisoning, particularly from lead
- Endangered status: no longer endangered

STOP AND THINK

Tell the Tale

Chapter Three describes what settlers thought of bald eagles. Imagine that you are a bald eagle whose habitat has become filled with settlers. In 200 words, write a story from the bald eagle's point of view. Describe the scene. Where would the eagle nest? How would it find food? Would there be any other challenges? Be sure to develop a sequence of events and include a conclusion.

Surprise Me

Chapter Two discusses characteristics of bald eagles. What three facts about bald eagles did you find most surprising? Write a few sentences about each fact. Why did you find each fact surprising?

Dig Deeper

After reading this book, what questions do you still have about why bald eagles were once an endangered species? With an adult's help, find a few reliable sources that can help you answer your questions. Write a paragraph about what you discover.

Say What?

Studying bald eagles can mean learning a lot of new vocabulary. Find five words in this book that you've never heard or seen before. Use a dictionary or the Internet to find out what they mean. Write down the meaning of each word. Then use each word in a new sentence.

GLOSSARY

bounty
an award of money given to a person for capturing or killing something

carrion
the flesh of a dead animal

conservation
preserving and protecting something

crop
a sac in an eagle's neck in which it can store food

DDT
a now-banned poison used to control pests that enters the food chain and harms the environment

habitat
a place in nature where animals or plants usually live

lead pellets
small balls used in shotguns that are made of lead

ornithologist
a scientist who studies birds

raptor
a bird that feeds on other animals

spawn
to produce or lay eggs in water

species
a group of animals or plants that share basic traits

LEARN MORE

Books

Blobaum, Cindy. *Explore Predators and Prey!: With 25 Great Projects*. White River Junction, VT: Nomad Press, 2016.

Dudley, Karen. *Bald Eagles*. New York: AV2 by Weigl, 2014.

McDowell, Pamela. *Bald Eagle*. New York: AV2 by Weigl, 2013.

Websites

To learn more about Back from Near Extinction, visit **booklinks.abdopublishing.com**. These links are routinely monitored and updated to provide the most current information available.

Visit **mycorelibrary.com** for free additional tools for teachers and students.

INDEX

ABOUT THE AUTHOR

Anita Yasuda is the author of more than 100 books for children. She enjoys writing biographies, books about science and social studies, and chapter books. Anita lives with her family in Huntington Beach, California, where she often walks her dog along the shore.